THANK YOU

Helen Westbrook

for all the years you have devoted to the
progress of education in our schools.

EDMONTON PUBLIC SCHOOLS

June, 1985   Chairman of the Board _Joan A. Cowling_

Superintendent of Schools _J. W. Bergmann_

CANADA

Land of many dreams

First published in Great Britain by Colour Library Books Ltd.
© 1983 Illustrations and text: Colour Library Books Ltd.,
   Guildford, Surrey, England.
First published in Canada by Royce Publications
Colour separations by FERCROM, Barcelona, Spain.
Display and text filmsetting by ACESETTERS Ltd., Richmond, Surrey, England.
Printed and bound in Barcelona, Spain by I.G. Domingo and Eurobinder.

ISBN O-86283-084-2
COLOUR LIBRARY BOOKS

Dep. Leg. B. 21.937/83

CANADA
Land of many dreams

Text by Robyn Johl

Produced by
TED SMART and DAVID GIBBON

Royce
PUBLICATIONS

Canada is a tapestry of majestic mountains, beautiful winding rivers and lakes, lush green forests and most of all a multi-cultural people.

As the second largest country in the world, Canada leaves the oldest homesteader still in awe of this land of diverse nature and topography.

Whether you travel more or less of the 4,665 miles of adventurous land, if you never leave Vancouver Island, you can explore and discover new nooks and crannies of pure delight and challenge. Every valley and village has its own unique geographical character – a landscape derived of man-made attractions and natural environment – a formal and wild design of man and nature coming together. Although Canada measures a total of 3.8 million square miles, second to Russia which is a total of 8.65 million square miles, Canada has just one-tenth of the population of the United States. This is mainly due to vast and uninhabited regions of the northern parts of Canada that is mostly tundra and solid polar ice that never thaws. The majority of Canada's population inhabits the southern regions, 250 miles north of the U.S.–Canada border.

From the rugged shorelines of the Atlantic provinces to the whitecapped waves of the Juan de Fuca Strait that run proudly into the Pacific Ocean, Canada is bursting with an environment that has been conquered by the bare hands of man to become one of the world's most progressive countries, worthy of recognition and a challenge to the generations to come.

Canada's twenty-three million inhabitants from all cultures and religions today stand proudly, identified as Canadians. Located next door to the world's greatest power, the United States, the "American" influence on the Canadian identity and economy has been a fact reluctantly acknowledged and it is with a strong sense of pride that Canadians have struggled to establish their own identity.

The common culture and language of the original people of the Americas made it difficult to differentiate the U.S. and Canada but over time the unique geography of this continent determined the differences. The natural resources, climate and especially the vastness of space forced the people to spread throughout the new land without unified loyalties to their mother country. Where the United States completely severed ties with Europe, Canada maintained loyalties to Great Britain. As a result of ugly wars and conflicts, the Americas were split by a simple U.S./Canada border line which runs almost straight across the middle of this huge continent separating the differences of the people and forcing them to settle in areas that predicted the character of the people, the architecture of their environment and customs of the land.

The original immigrants go back as far as 8000 B.C. – prehistoric man, and because there is no written historical proof, it is only a theory that the Indians were originally mongols from Asia. The Nordics braved the waters of the unknown world much later – some historians claim it was as late as the 16th century. Folk tales and legends were spread throughout Europe of the abundance of fish in the Atlantic waters and the sparsely inhabited land of wilderness. Hence the coming of the white man and his tools.

Today, Canada stands "north strong and free," just as the national anthem states. On April 17, 1982 the final ties of protocol with Britain were broken by bringing home the Canadian Constitution. Although Canadians have practised self-government and total autonomy for 56 years the British North American Act of 1867, in effect the Constitution of Canada, could only be amended by the British Parliament. Therefore, every time Canada wanted to make a change in its own constitution, it needed the final consent of British Parliament.

It was not until 1980 when a very determined Prime Minister, Pierre Trudeau, and his government were able to strengthen the constitution by including a Bill of Rights and transfer the document to Canada. In April 1982, Queen Elizabeth II officially brought it back to Canada.

Canada's rich environment and valuable natural resources are envied throughout the world. Politically, economically and socially, Canada is one of the most stable countries in the world and is a desirable destination for both new immigrants and holiday makers.

No man is an island. Canada respects and is still a member of the British Commonwealth and will continue to be involved. Britain and the United States are, with mutual respect, necessary allies to Canada. Not only for its geographic proximity but for their common belief in western democracy and respect for the inherent rights and freedoms of all people. Very few foreign policies or agreements are made without consulting with these important allies and friends.

Canada is an unforgettable experience. No other country can boast of such diversity of wilderness and peaceful, calm landscapes. From the eastern Maritime and Newfoundland provinces to the commercial capitals of Ontario and Quebec, across the wide open wheat fields of the prairies to the equally unique western provinces of Alberta and British Columbia, Canada is full of differences and a sameness. The never forgotten Yukon and Northwest Territories still challenge and delight the explorer, while the Hollywood moviemakers and holiday makers take advantage of the profound scenery and challenging sports.

It may seem quite amazing, but history records the Indian population as far back as the 16th century to be approximately 220,000. The 1978 consensus shows only 302,749 Indians registered under the Indian Act of Canada. Only a detailed history of the Americas can explain this lack of increase. However, a simple explanation is the coming of the white man and his determination to invade, develop and progress in a country so new, vast and rich, which in the end defeated the growth of the indigenous people of America.

Originally, the Indians of Canada were divided into five main groups including the Inuit who are popularly known as Eskimos, and were spread throughout the Canadian wilderness. Each tribe or group was distinguishable by the regions they inhabited and the manner of their dress, livelihood and size of groups. The Inuit were isolated to the northern regions of the Arctic and remain there to this day.

Their basic needs of food, clothing and shelter determined their travels and settlements. For these purposes effective tools of survival were invented and made with the rawest of materials such as shaven rock or bones of animals. Wood and bark of trees were used for making canoes and animal skins for clothing, teepees and wigwams. Beaded crafts were made of shells and bones while on tree trunks they carved their legends and stories of victories, romance, hunting conquests and superstition. Snow-shoes and sleds made their winter travels possible while dogs and horses were trained to master the harsh winters and wilderness. Crafty weapons and traps were made to aid their survival. Bows and arrows and inventive traps were all they needed to hunt their buffalo, to catch their wild rabbits and fish and to defend themselves against their enemy – man or beast.

The Algonquins were the most nomadic breed of Indian, located mostly in eastern Canada. The people were split up into different tribes such as the Algonquins of the Ottawa-St. Lawrence area, Micmacs of the Maritimes, Mongagnais of Quebec and Cree and Ojibwa of Northern Ontario and Manitoba.

The Iroquois were mainly farmers and settled around the fertile land of St. Lawrence Valley and the Great Lakes. This was a proud tribe and its strength was in numbers and loyalty as a unified group. It was, therefore, an influential and fearsome tribe. They grew tobacco, squash and pumpkins and most importantly, the Indian corn and maize. They lived in houses made of logs and took pride in the craftsmanship of their beaded jewelry and pottery for trade with other tribes and later to bargain with the white man.

The Sioux, Blackfeet, and Cree were similar to the Algonquins in that they were nomads and the nature of Canada determined their lifestyle. They wandered north from Mexico and with them they brought horses. They adapted the horse to the nature of the land and the horse became as necessary to them for survival as the tools of our survival today. With the horse they travelled and hunted and conquered the wilderness and the indeterminate climate.

The Haida, Nootka and Salish tribes of the Pacific discovered the bounties of mountain streams and coastal waters. The huge timbers and plentiful salmon kept them content for generations.

The climate, wilderness and the unknown were overcome by this indigenous group of Canadians. They needed no maps, compasses or riches to purchase unknown luxuries.

The coming of the white man was inevitable with the age of Renaissance and discovery and the increased scientific knowledge of the Europeans. Christopher Columbus had reached the Americas, European commerce was expanding and the curiosity of the eastern riches were arousing the interest of the wealthy traders and businessmen.

In search of the eastern riches men discovered the Americas and soon the riches of the Americas. By the middle of the 16th century the whole eastern coast of North America had been touched by the white man and the New World was open to all (Spanish, Portuguese, French, English and Irish), including the Christian missionaries who were determined to convert these pagan Indians to Christianity.

With the discovery of the plentiful cod fish all round Newfoundland, Gulf of St. Lawrence, Cape Breton Island and Nova Scotia, came the discovery of the beaver pelt. The English and French soon realized the value of fur bearing animals in this New World and learned to trade a few trinkets and knives for pelts to be sold in Europe for huge profits.

To this day, fishing is one of the most important industries of Canada but it was the fur trade that motivated the Europeans to move deeper into the wilderness and eventually to the Pacific coast of Canada. With the help of the original fur hunters, the Indians, the white man learned to survive and hunt in the Canadian wilderness. The beaver is still a national Canadian symbol.

Although the exploitation of the Indian cannot be denied, miraculously they survived. Today there are 575 Indian bands living on different reserves throughout Canada. There are fifty-eight different Indian languages belonging to ten major linguistic groups: the Algonquin, Iroquois, Sioux, Athabaskan, Kootenayan, Salishan, Wakashan, Tsimshian, Haida and Tlingit. The Indians are protected by the Federal and Provincial levels of government through the Department of Indian Affairs and Northern Development. Their culture and craftsmanship is preserved in museums and art galleries throughout Canada. Their wood and soapstone carvings are prized all over the world. Totem poles are commissioned by

the Orient and Europeans, especially in the West, who are reminded of their true heritage. The Indian dances, customs and dress are both symbolic and entertaining to the modern man and a colourful fascination to children and adult alike. Due to various government programs such as self-help workshops, education grants and heightening their social awareness, many successful entrepreneurs and community leaders have emerged. Successful land claim settlements have provided the Indians with a choice of life in cities or the more traditional lifestyle.

The Inuit (Eskimos) are a fascinating group of native Canadians who number only 23,000. Although they no longer live in igloos, they remain close to their original habitat and livelihood. They are spread thoughout the northern regions of the Arctic islands, Northwest Territories, Labrador and the shores of Hudson Bay, where the ways of the southern man has invaded the northern communities. Electricity, snowmobiles, trucks, schools, hospitals, films and television have all changed northern life.

With the help of government grants, more and more Inuit are receiving education and professional skills and trades. Gone are the sled dogs and here to stay are the motorized toboggans.

For long journeys and emergencies the airplane is the Arctic taxi. World War II also brought about changes to decrease the vast space between the northern regions and the more civilized south. The building of defence installations and of meteorological and radio stations brought reliable communications and development of the northern environment.

With the developments, however, evolved the concerns for Inuit interests, especially for their land and the preservation of Inuit lifestyle and culture. Associations and agreements between the Inuit and Federal government developed and the Inuit are now represented in the territorial, provincial and federal level of government including an elected Inuk member in the House of Commons.

The story of Canada is as diverse as the beauty and magnificence of this land. The trader, lumberman, farmer, industrialist and banker evolved from the man wearing feathers and skins and beaver pelt hats.

Canada is split into ten provinces, the Northwest Territory and the Yukon – each with its unique cultural, political, and social background, and landscape. The similarity in the provinces is in their national pride. The preservation of Canadian heritage and culture and their natural environment, while maintaining progressive attitudes towards change and development is the back bone of the new Canadian. This is what makes Canada interesting and unique. It is a country still young and unspoiled, a place where one can still feel close to the smells, tastes and emotions of nature, where blue skies, pure rivers and year round green forests are untouched by man, while modern technology has provided Canadians with one of the highest standards of living in the world.

Canadian history began in Atlantic Canada which includes four provinces: Nova Scotia, New Brunswick, Prince Edward Island and Newfoundland. The combined area of these provinces is just over twice that of the United Kingdom with a total population less than that of Wales.

Newfoundland was the first settlement and closest landmark to its ancestors. The island was discovered in 1497 by John Cabot, sailing under the British flag. The oldest street of North America, known as Water Street, runs through St. John's, the capital city of Newfoundland and the oldest and busiest seaport of Atlantic Canada.

One can easily conjure a picturesque province of fishing villages, built within rugged, rocky shorelines populated with sea worn faces of a mixed population of English, French and Irish, who originally settled to establish a fishing port. Fish meant cod and there was plenty of it. Traders from France and Britain came and went loaded with rich cod as did the Americans. With no laws of the sea to protect the few settlers, it became evident to the European merchants that some forms of propriety and laws had to be founded. The struggles of imperialism began – mainly between the French and English. It was not until 1904 that France gave up her rights to land on the valuable western front and 1910 that American fishermen were prohibited from complete freedom of unlimited fish claims. Newfoundland finally had full control of its own fisheries. The valuable railway lines were built with the aid of government grants and with this progress came farmers, mining and lumber products, pulp and paper mills. While these industries brought new wealth, the province needed manpower and financial aid for public works and social service programmes. The two World Wars had hit Newfoundland's population hard, as did the Great Depression of the thirties, which ran the province into bankruptcy. Newfoundland was important because of its proximity to Europe and, therefore, became a strategic naval base for both Canada and the United States, bringing people, money and status to the province. It was British capital that put Newfoundland back on its feet and it was this dependency and gratitude that made Newfoundland reluctant to join the Canadian Confederacy. The last of the British colonial connections to Canada was not severed until 1949 when Newfoundland was the tenth and last province to join the other Confederate provinces.

Separated by the narrow Strait of Belle Isle, Labrador is valuable Newfoundland territory. Although it still remains an isolated region, it handles the bulk of Canada's iron ore and hydro-electric power. It is part of the oldest section of the Canadian Shield that surrounds Hudson Bay. The Grand Banks are one of the richest cod fishing grounds of the world while Notre Dame Bay is popular for tuna and Gander for salmon fishing.

The Newfoundlanders have preserved their wild life with bird sanctuaries at Witless Bay, Bird Island and Cape St. Mary while herds of caribou can be found roaming the Trepassey Barrens. All around the Avalon Peninsula you can find fishing villages, with quaint English names, where fish nets are thrown out for drying or repair and fisherman clean the catch of the day. Cape Spear National Historic Park is a monument to World War II where caves were used to store armaments for the allied armed forces.

The modern Trans-Canada Highway running coast to coast gives access to most of the scenic fishing villages and national parks of Newfoundland. Gander became a major international airport after World War II and commemorates its memorable history with an Aviation Museum. The beautiful Terra Nova National Park is just east of Gander.

Beaver, muskrat, red fox, lynx and Canada geese can be found along the nature trails while the provincial flower, the carnivorous pitcher plant grows in inland peat bogs.

West of Notre Dame Bay is the important mining industry of copper, silver, gold, lead, zinc, cadmium, and asbestos. Rock collectors can find beauties of all configurations around the peninsula.

As the first inhabitants of Canada, it is not surprising that nearly ninety-five per cent of the Newfoundlanders today were born on the island. A short ferry ride away are the islands of St. Pierre and Miquelon which are French territories and therefore totally French in character. St. Pierre is one of the oldest European towns in North America and is popular with the American tourists.

Along the shorelines of the Great Northern Peninsula is the Gros Morne National Park, which has some of the most spectacular fjords in North America. This 750-square mile park of phenomenal scenery is a curious mixture of volcanic origins, deep fjords on the Gulf of St. Lawrence and wooded trails. From the top of Gros Morne is a magnificent view of the sea and rugged tundra. The hiking trails can surprise you with the sight of black bear, moose, otter, beaver, caribou or even a bald eagle.

The first transatlantic wireless message sent by Marchese Guglielmo Marconi in 1901 was to St. John's and the event is recorded in Signal Hill Historic Park. A drive along Prince Phillip Drive leads to Confederation Hill and Confederation Building houses the Military Museum. St. John's is a delightful treat. The fine restaurants of European cuisine as well as all the local fresh fish dishes are a true sign of the heritage of the people and the influx of immigrants since the pioneer days.

The Atlantic shores include the quiet gardens of Prince Edward Island. Nestled between Cape Breton Island and the shores of New Brunswick, Prince Edward Island is a picture of a peaceful resort island. Rolling green hills, sandy beaches and potato fields characterize the environment of Canada's smallest province of 2,184 square miles. The sports fishermen are never disappointed for a bluefin tuna.

Charlottetown, the capital city of the island, is proud of its historic buildings, period churches and colonial seaport. A statement to the easy atmosphere of this province is the core of the city, with the beautiful 40-acre Victoria Park overlooking the harbour. The Confederation Centre of the Arts is the focal point and houses a national museum, art gallery and theatre. The famous theatre production of Anne of Green Gables, a story of a pigtailed orphan who grew up in rural Prince Edward Island, is held annually during the summer festival. Blue Heron Drive, though only a 25 mile stretch, will take you through beautiful national parks and beaches to New London Bay where blue herons run about freely.

Prince Edward Island has much to offer. There are many restored historical sites as well as modern restaurants with tasty cuisines to suit the most hearty and connoisseur tastes. Prince Edward Island National Park is an incredible scene of sheer awesome beauty. More than 250 species of birds can be found here, as well as the great blue herons. Weather worn rock formations line the miles of sea shore dunes. The park begins at Tracadie Bay and Dalway Beach and ends up at Cavendish Bay. Cavendish is best known for being the setting for Lucy Maud Montgomery's novel *Anne of Green Gables*. Though the paths that Anne explored have been turned into a golf course, the marks of Lover's Lane, the Babbling Brook, the Haunted Woods, and the Lake of Shining Waters can still be seen while the country farmhouse in which Anne grew up in is a popular tourist attraction.

The western coast of Prince Edward Island is the home of Acadians, descendents of French settlers of the seventeenth century. Their music, dancing and food is traditional, as is their speech and religion.

Throughout the Maritimes, colourful county fairs depict the history, culture and customs with pride. Festivals are held in honour of the abundance of their natural foods such as the Oyster Festival and Potato Blossom Festival.

Samuel de Champlain landed on the Fundy shore of Nova Scotia in 1604 and it was here that Sieur de Monts, founded the first successful French settlement in North America.

However it did not take long for the English to become intimidated by the French settlements and they took serious action when the French built the Fortress of Louisbourg as a strategic hold on Cape Breton Island. The Royal Navy, once again, won the battle of the day.

The news of the New World's wealth spread and thus began an influx of more Europeans. The Germans came and settled on the southwest shores of Nova Scotia, next came the Loyalists after the American Revolution, starving shiploads of Irish came leaving their homelands during the potato famine of the 1840's; the Scots came and settled at Pitcou county on the northwestern shore and at Cape Breton with its highland-like glens.

Today, Nova Scotia thrives as the core of the Maritime provinces. Halifax is the capital of Nova Scotia and the commercial and military centre of the four Maritime provinces.

Even for its multi-cultural population, Nova Scotia maintains its small town atmosphere with its tree-lined streets, stately Georgian buildings and busy pubs.

A major naval base, the harbours are lined with submarines, frigates and destroyers. The fish boats and freighters are a busy scene and assure the bystanders of the peaceful gracious hospitality of the people. Handmade arts and crafts and old-county humour and folk songs display the cultural heritage and pride of these Atlantic provinces. The country hoe-downs, fiddling contests, International Gathering of the Clans, Hometown celebrations and food festivals are just a few ways in which their heritage and character is alive and well.

The modern resort and convention facilities surrounded by spectacular scenic surroundings are a sign of progress well planned not to spoil the environment but to spoil the visitor with beautiful golf grounds, with easy access to fishing and with swimming on sandy beaches. The Keltic Lodge, Digby Pines and Liscombe Lodge are just a few developments run by the Nova Scotia government. The Nova Scotians take great pride in restoring historic properties such as the Fort Anne National Historic Park. The history of this 28-acre park goes back to the scenes of attacks on the fort by the English, the French, New Englanders, Indians, and even pirates.

Historic museums represent replicas of their ancestor's struggles and achievements while Alexander Graham Bell, a born Scotsman and inventor of the telephone, is commemorated in a museum near his summer house on Cape Breton Island.

A natural setting for nature lovers, the Maritimes are a popular getaway for contemplative thought, reading, writing, painting and the arts. Nova Scotia's Kejimkujik National Park, just southwest of Halifax is ideal for hiking and canoeing along old Micmac Indian trails. Cape Breton Highlands National Park is surrounded by unforgettable rugged scenery reminding the locals of their Scottish ancestry. Freshwater fishing is a popular sport where Atlantic salmon and speckled trout are plentiful as well as saltwater groundfish such as cod, mackerel and pollac.

Every little cove, historic park or village has its interesting story and the Maritime provinces are full of untold and sometimes mysterious tales of the original settlers of Canada. A living example of the great seafaring voyages is the *Bluenose II*, a replica of the original Bluenose ships that the Maritimes depended on for their trade and livelihood.

The American Revolution drove many United Empire Loyalists (settlers from American colonies who remained loyal to Britain during the Revolution) northwards. Many settled in the province of New Brunswick.

Although this extensive seacoast invited the fishermen and seafaring man, it was the lumbering and shipbuilding facility that the British market needed to replenish their wartime deficits. By 1800 lumbering had joined the fur trade as one of the main activities of the British North American colonies and New Brunswick became one of the biggest shipbuilding centres in the British Empire.

Located in the Gulf of St. Lawrence, just under the Gaspé Peninsula, Prince Edward Island enjoys rich agricultural land, green forests, and mineral resources.

Today thirty-five per cent of the population is Acadian. The major urban areas are important Canadian distribution and manufacturing centres, and they are primary to the economy of New Brunswick. Fredericton is the capital of the province and has a large populace of artists as well as historical arts and craft shops and museums. At Kings Landing Historical Settlement "villages" are recreated to display scenes of people in traditional costume churning butter, making soap and spinning and weaving their yarn. The Kings Head Inn is a popular place to stop for nineteenth century foods while the Loyalist and French traditions are celebrated with the same zeal of their forefathers.

The bulk of this province is made up of incredible landscapes of lush forests and seascapes. The tides at the Bay of Fundy are the highest in the world and cause the reversing falls of Saint John. A natural phenomena that can only be believed by seeing.

The Acadian Trail is a 270 mile drive from Shediac where the famous Lobster Festival is held each year. The trail is a historical life story of the Micmac Indian and the French settlements. It features picturesque fishing villages and national parks.

The Fundy Trail personifies the characteristics of the people who remained loyal to the Crown. Besides the awesome tides of this southern coast, the area is famous for its challenging deep sea fishing. It was also the summer home of Franklin D. Roosevelt at Campobello. The Fundy National Park is the place for canoeing, hiking and fishing. St. Stephen is approximately ten miles from the U.S./Canada border, crossing into the State of Maine, and is known for one of the great joys of life today, the chocolate bar. After eighty years, the Ganong Brothers Ltd. are still churning out the candy.

The famous seaside resort, St. Andrews, is where golfers, writers and artists are inspired by unforgettable scenic landscapes. The Rossmount Inn, set in a wildlife sanctuary, has served presidents and prime ministers with mouth watering menus that include salmon, pollock, lobster and fiddlehead soup (the curled-up fronds of the ostrich fern which are becoming the unofficial symbol of New Brunswick).

The Kouchibouguac National Park is a popular bathing area with twenty-five miles of sand dunes.

Whitewater canoeing in the Saint John River is a challenging sport while visiting Edmundston near the United States border of Maine. One of the central features of this Acadian town is the Roman Catholic Cathedral of the Immaculate Conception. The spires of the church can be seen from all over the city.

The mighty St. Lawrence river flows south to the Great Lakes and has always been the heart of Canadian settlement. The rich farmlands and industrial resources were the incentive and today the two largest commercial cities of Canada, Toronto and Montreal are located in this region. Events in history determined and divided the people as the French settled mainly in what is now the province of Quebec while the British tended to settle in Upper Canada, now known as Ontario.

In 1534 a man, still searching for the passage to India, sailed into the Gulf of St. Lawrence. It was at Stadacona that Jacques Cartier met the Algonquin Indians, who told him he was in Kanata or Canada. The harsh rapids of the St. Lawrence stopped his voyage at the village of Hochelaga where he was forced to turn back after passing the mountain crest Mount Royal, today known as Montreal.

The roots of the French settlements were laid and they conquered this land of wilderness and natural resources. The coureur-des-bois who were famous for their "Indian sense," learned to track and hunt with the instincts of their native Canadian teachers and trekked on to challenge the new world. The efforts of Champlain, the missionaries and pioneers laid their mark as land was cleared and settlements were formed.

The province of Quebec began with sporadic fur trading settlements and went on to become one of the commercial centres of Canada for European and American trade. The rich farmlands, industry, and hydro-electric power together with unsurpassed scenic beauty and geography make up this unique province. Quebec is a proud testimony to past and present Canada, with eighty per cent of its population

French speaking. The old and new Quebec City is the capital of Quebec, surrounded by remarkable coastal scenery. It stands, nobly surrounded by its stone walled Citadel fortress, with original cannons, churches, cobbled streets and quaint homes and restaurants that make one feel like you have stepped into a little piece of sixteenth century France. The majestic Chateau Frontenac and the modern Hilton complement one another, while first class winter and summer resorts are popular pleasure spots.

One of the most exciting cosmopolitan cities in North America is Montreal. Its European flair of old and modern sophistication has made it the fashion capital of Canada. International events such as Expo '67, World Olympics and conferences have made Quebec a popular destination for visitors and business. Whether it is sophisticated culture and entertainment, dining, professional sports (especially ice-hockey and football), or wilderness hunting and fishing or playing golf on splendid green courses, Quebec has it. Challenging ski slopes at luxury resorts such as St. Sauveur and Mount Tremblant are just a few hours drive north of Montreal in the well known Laurentian Mountains.

One of Quebec's major industrial cities is Trois Rivieres, located at the mouth of the St. Maurice River, where rich timberlands are a staple of local industry. The St. Maurice Valley is one of the most beautiful areas of Quebec and includes the De la Mauricie National Park, a 200 square mile park of wonderland. The park begins at Lac la Peche and the canoe is the only feasible means of transportation to the wilderness campsites located on any of the sixty lakes and many rivers. The sandy beaches are contrasted by the glacier-torn mountainsides. The St. Maurice Reserve is a reminder, to the Quebecois and visitor, of Canada's wild mountains, rivers and woods.

Ontario is obvious in its British heritage with cities, streets, restaurants, and rivers with English names such as York, London, Stratford, Avon and Windsor. Toronto prides itself as being the New York City of Canada and the modern skyscrapers, sophisticated arts and cultural centres equal that of any busy cosmopolitan city, but with a difference – it is typically Canadian, clean, hospitable, safe and beautiful. The melting pot of diverse cultures and religions, Ontario has a large Chinese and Italian population with smaller communities of French, German, and East Indians. Communities have built up over the generations to form proud unified Canadian identities with individual cultures, religions and customs. Some of the best writers, artists, sports stars, and academics have come out of the progressive province. The hub of big business has won Toronto the reputation of being the commercial and financial capital of Canada.

Ottawa, capital city of Canada and the home of central government, is one of the prettiest cities in Ontario. Rideau Canal runs through the middle of tree-lined streets to Parliament Hill. Energetic people ice-skate to work along the winding canal in the winter while in the summer a common scene is a colourful array of boats. The heart of Ottawa is the Parliament Buildings, but for enjoyment and culture the first class National Arts Centre has some of the finest Canadian and International art collections in Canada.

British architecture and culture is represented throughout Ontario in many forms. Stratford on the River Avon is the site of the annual Shakespeare Festival and is famous for its artistic excellence. Not far from Stratford is the "Forest City," London. Running through the heart of London is the Thames River which flows through one of the oldest university campuses in Canada, The University of Western Ontario, and through Springbank Park where a cruise on the Thames can be had on the paddlewheeler "Storybook Queen."

The rich southern region is Ontario's tobacco belt and mixed farmlands. The city of Windsor and its sister city, Detroit, which is just across the United States border, are the centres of automotive industry in Canada and the United States.

The famous Niagara Falls are also shared by Canada's neighbour. Plunging over 200 feet down limestone cliffs, the Niagara River is split into three – the American Falls, the Horseshoe (Canadian) Falls and a smaller fall, Bridal Veil, on the American side. The Indians originally called the falls Onigara, "thunder of waters," and often sacrificed beautiful maidens over the falls. Hence the legend of a "maid in the mist," which is perpetuated today by a boat by the same name that caters to the tourists who want to venture close to the falls at ground level.

From urban sophistication to frontier land, through "English counties" such as Essex and Kent, and across the harsh, mineral-rich mining districts of the Canadian Shield, through the trapping and fur country and north of the Great Lakes, Ontario is a mosaic of ethnic and cultural diversity.

From natural recreational centres, to sophisticated resorts in the Muskokas or a historical trip on the Polar Bear Express across the wide Arctic from Cochrane to remote isolated Moosonee, one can experience a blend of Nature's and man's genius. Near the mouth of Moose River on James Bay, Ontario has some incredible sights to see, such as a trading post built in the 1670's by the Hudson Bay Company which still stands with plaques and museums to tell the saga of French and British battles.

Science, technology, world competitive manufacturing and first class arts and culture make Canada proud of Ontario's growth and developments. The CN Tower, the world's largest free standing structure, is a noble landmark facing east to west and overseas, acknowledging the people of the world that made this achievement possible.

The prairie provinces of Manitoba, Saskatchewan and Alberta stretch as far west as the Rocky Mountains and north to the Arctic. Producing 79% of Canada's farm products, the plains region has a dubious image of flat lands. Endless miles of grain-producing land conjures a painter's picture of golden wheat fields over vast empty spaces. However, the "bread basket of the world" also has its share of park lands, green forests, large lakes and, in the southern areas of Alberta and Saskatchewan, the cowboys are cattle ranching, and the more recently discovered rich oil resources in Alberta have made Alberta the pride and envy of the rest of Canada.

Manitoba, bordered by the U.S. state of North Dakota, was named by its original inhabitants, the Ojibwa Indians. After the British, the major immigrant groups to this region are the Mennonites, Icelanders and Ukrainians.

Restored forts and museums are formal proof of how little time has changed the people in isolated areas and how unspoiled the country still is.

The internationally acclaimed Winnipeg Ballet Company is the pride of Canada, while the diverse cultural activities of Winnipeg feed the vitality of this city as much as the winding Red and Assiniboine rivers that run through the commercial centre of modern skyscrapers.

Another isolated prairie province is Saskatchewan and it is here that the original Royal Canadian Mounted Police Headquarters began to symbolize the important part this territory played in Canada's history. A small group of peace-makers started rallying for the protection of the Indians and maintaining law and order in remote wilderness and the west. Originally known as the Northwest Mounted Police, their deeds and brave episodes became a symbol of Canadian law and order. Today Regina is the centre for training new recruits and the Mounted Police are renowned for their excellent horsemanship, their proud red-coated uniform and is a most appropriate Canadian symbol of tradition and justice.

Moose Jaw, Swift Current, Saskatoon – every inch of the land has a unique story to tell . . . how the harsh winters were survived, how the women's suffragettes began, how the railways and Trans-Canada highway began building the economy of Canada and unifying its people. The friendly border towns today celebrate the differences and the friendly dependencies – for trade, tourism and cultural exchange.

The province of Alberta has an identity all its own. Nowhere is the Indian heritage more proudly presented. The Texas-like image of cowboys, oil prosperity and rich Indian culture has given Alberta a natural western image. The home of the famous Calgary Stampede, the majestic Rocky Mountains, and scenic resorts cannot be duplicated anywhere else in the world. Nestled between majestic mountains is Banff – featuring the popular Canadian Pacific Banff Springs Hotel, Banff School of Fine Arts, Lake Louise, Jasper Park and Conservation Parks and ski slopes which are world renowned. One has to wonder in awe of the toil of the men who built the railways and highways through this breath-takingly rugged land of overwhelming snow capped mountains, freezing mountain rivers and twisting canyons. Not overnight, but gradually, the challenge of this land was met and the western gates to the Pacific Ocean were opened.

The immense Rocky Mountain range is one of the world's greatest natural borders stretching from the Yukon Territory through the United States to New Mexico. The 200 mile long stretch that borders Alberta and British Columbia contains some of the finest mountain scenery of the world.

Fort Edmonton is a re-creation of Alberta's history located just outside of Edmonton, the capital city of Alberta. Battles between Indian tribes are remembered by preservation of forts and old towns while the legendary stories of gold prospecting and pioneering days are celebrated during Klondike Days. The Waterton Lakes National Park is a more ancient part of the Rockies encompassing beautiful, clear lakes and mountain streams full of fresh water trout. The Cypress Hills Provincial Park, a desert-like phenomena, surrounds the dinosaur-ridden badlands and the Blackfoot Indian Reserve where Indian history and traditions are told. John Ware's cabin is a museum depicting life of an early Alberta rancher who was a former slave from South Carolina and in the early 1800's came to the Red Deer River Valley and eventually took up cattle ranching in this rich valley.

From discoveries of dinosaur skeletons to the discovery of rich mineral resources and the more recent oil discoveries, Alberta's city of Calgary is booming with big business and developments. Today "Whooping-Up" is displayed with celebrations of Indian traditions, stetson hats, chuckwagon races, kegs of beer and rodeo features. The province is Britain in inheritance but western Canadian in culture, character and environment.

After the last spike was driven in 1885 at Craigellachie, British Columbia, the east-west Canadian Pacific Railway was completed and a dream which began twenty-two years ago in Charlottetown, Newfoundland was witnessed by Sir John A. Macdonald. A feat completed in five years has decades of stories to tell. The unification of Canada became a physical reality but British Columbia, being situated on the Pacific Ocean, developed trade markets to a different world, the Far East and Japan.

The gold rush brought settlers to this rich province from all over the world. However, it is the lumber, mining and fishing industries that sustain the economy of this super, natural province today. Dairy farming, mixed farming and fruit growing are the staples of this rich, fertile land. Blessed with some of the most scenic sights in the world, this young, resource rich province has an identity all its own.

The proximity to the United States made British Columbia accessible to American influences and trade and the Peace Arch Station that stands between the State of Washington and British Columbia is symbolic of a common heritage and friendliness.

The history of British Columbia like the rest of Canada has been influenced by its Indian heritage and its geography. The immense wilderness forced the population to be centered in the southwest on Vancouver Island and the lower mainland. The Okanagan Valley is a rich fruit growing region and is situated amongst the prettiest lake scenery of the province. This mixed terrain is horseriding country and a naturalist's delight. Deer, moose, grizzly bear, caribou and elk can be seen roaming around the Cascade and Monaskee Mountains. The Indians found plenty of soap stone, jade and agate in this area for their splendid works of traditional art. The tallest totem pole in the world stands as a noble testimonial to history, tradition and the nature of British Columbia.

No other province can boast the beauty of the setting of snow capped mountains, lush green forests and innumerable lakes and streams. The rivers and white water rapids run wildly through serene wilderness to be enjoyed for their sheer luxury and ruggedness.

Vancouver has a unique personality made up of yet another group of immigrants. Like the name of the province, it is British in heritage but it is proud of its ethnic diversity. It has the largest and oldest population of Chinese, outside San Francisco, who came to the new world to help build Canada's railways. The Chinese are today some of the wealthiest merchants and entrepreneurs of Canada, adding to the mosaic land a rich and exotic culture. The East Indians from India, as they had to be called to differentiate them from the indigenous Indians, are a part of British Columbia's history rarely told. The lumber and pulp and paper mills prospered under the labour of these people and today much of this industry is owned and worked by these people. The rich farmlands around the Fraser Valley is also dominated by these industrious people. The new generation Canadians are pursuing higher education and contribute to all facets of Canadian society.

Vancouver is the third largest city in Canada and is surrounded by spectacular scenery of mountains and by leisure and industrial waterways. The English Bay lines the shorelines of beautiful, year round green Stanley Park, with sandy beaches. Avid sailors, windsurfers and water skiers enjoy the changeable scenery around this seven mile park. Burrard Inlet is an active harbour for ocean going freighters and luxury cruise liners. The man-made False Creek surrounds Granville Island where an inventive imagination created open air fruit and produce markets, Arts Club, and pubs and restaurants with unique atmospheres overlooking the pleasure boats and skyscrapers that line the opposite shore of Vancouver's city centre and the location of Expo '86. Expansive bridges link the metropolitan city centre to the popular ski resorts such as Grouse and Seymour Mountains and the North Shore that takes you along the scenic drive of British Properties, Capilano Canyon, through to Horseshoe Bay, Squamish and Whistler Village. In the opposite direction is the picturesque Deep Cove and, after crossing the Second Narrows Bridge into Burnaby, the Simon Fraser University can be found uniquely situated on top of Burnaby Mountain. Its architecture design has invited international acclaim and interest.

A short ferry ride from Tsawassen through the Strait of Georgia and past picturesque Gulf Islands, you arrive at Victoria on Vancouver Island. Victoria practices all the traditions of Ye Olde England. High teas are served at the harbour front Empress Hotel, flower baskets add colour to the cobbled street nooks and crannies of antique shops and English China shops. Catering to the American tourists they even have a double decker bus to take the visitors around the Monte Carlo-like coastline. Famous for its gardens, the island takes great pride in keeping the parks and environment beautiful and picturesque. The famous Butchart Gardens is thirty acres of native and exotic flowers including the Japanese, English and Italian gardens.

The northern parts of Vancouver Island are a reminder of the Indian inhabitants with places like Duncan, Nanaimo, Port Alberni and Courtenay. Handmade crafts and Cowichan Indian sweaters can be bought in most souvenir shops along the island. The locals are more interested in the industry that booms in the areas. Coal, lumber and fishing are rich resources of the Island. Campbell River is a mining and lumbering port but its fame is for its excellent salmon fishing.

The lower mainland of British Columbia boasts of mild winters and although it can rain a lot, a common scene of sail boats, golfers, and hearty sea-wall walkers and joggers can be seen in the middle of winter. Most of the resorts are capitalizing on the weather to call themselves "Four Season" resorts. New developments, such as Whistler, cater to the year-round visitor or locals who like to get away from the city on a weekend.

While provincial museums and art galleries preserve their heritage, the Parliament Buildings determine the future of British Columbia. New developments continue as new coal resources are cultivated and still new townships are created. The history and legends spread north to Dawson Creek, Prince George, Fort St. John and the Northwest Territories. From Vancouver, the "Prince George" takes holidaymakers on an unforgettable Alaskan cruise. Life of the "old days" is restored in places such as Barkerville where the 1862 gold digger, Billy Barker, discovered his fortune of gold. The hub of prospectors is today a ghost town for tourists.

Yesterday and today proudly blend in beautiful British Columbia to give its people an identity of their own.

Across the northern border of Canada's provinces are the Northwest and Yukon Territories. This region accounts for one-third of Canada's total area. A truer test of conquering the elements of the unknown nature of Canada could not have been met save for the character and determination of the people who came and stayed. The Indians and Inuit adapted the vast wilderness and the harshest climatic elements by hunting wild caribou, bears, moose and elk as a way of life.

Torn between the technological advancement of modern

man and the traditional way of life, the Inuit and Indians have been forced to choose between accepting the urbanized lifestyle, centred in Yellowknife of the Northwest Territories and Whitehorse of the Yukon Territory or struggling to maintain a lifestyle based on the land as yet untouched by modern development.

Oil and mining discoveries have had their effect on the environment but there is still plenty of unexploited land that will allow the Inuit and Indians to choose their way of life. The necessity for education and social programs including health protection have been recognised by both the government and the people and are now widely available.

The Trail of '98 takes you through the challenging, memorable Yukon Territory and through history itself. The many legends of the Klondike Days, the days of the gold rush, are told and covered while trekking through wild and wanderous land along frozen Yukon River, ghost towns, and untouched elements of nature. Artifacts and signs mark the Trail: steps carved in ice at Chilkoot Pass, a suspension bridge across the Taiya River, man-made handrails along steep climbs, while man's invention of the train or boat down Yukon River completes the journey to Dawson City. The Trail of '98 is a 500 mile trek of history and nature's beauty at its wildest and most serene.

From Great Slave Lake to the Nahanni National Park in the Southwestern corner of the Northwest Territories, there are nearly two thousand miles of hiking on land of mountains and lakes and some of the purest and wildest stretches of white water in the world. From the thunderous waterfalls to wild orchids and sulphur hot springs, to the awesome manifestations of the Northern Lights, the Territories are an unforgettable experience.

The story of Canada has only just begun. From the wilderness Trail of '98 to the modern Trans-Canada Highway that stretches across some of the most beautiful scenery in the world, Canada has myriads of stories and untold legends that culminate in the reality that Canadians have come a long way.

This vast land can today be covered by Canada's national airline, Air Canada, from Halifax to Vancouver in six hours, nearly the same as the distance from Britain to Toronto. The Canadian Pacific Railway was built in five years and today it takes Via Rail a mere five days to cover the territory between Montreal and Vancouver. Major international airports link the rest of the world to Canada with major airlines such as Air Canada, Canadian Pacific Airlines and Wardair who offer scheduled and charter rates. Their importance is not only in transporting people but in the import/export of cargo to all parts of the world.

Canada today enjoys an envious position in world affairs, thanks to the dedication, and determination of Canadians. Canada has proudly produced its share of heroes – in war, sports, education, science and technology and the fine and performing arts.

People of every race, creed and colour live in this multicultural garden. However, the beauty of the people is their common bond as a proud Canadian.

Canada is a photographer's challenge and delight and the essence of this book is a pictorial tribute to Canada's history, the people, and its geographic phenomena . . . a wild, serene and colourful land, so majestic in its natural beauty and elegance.

When the first explorers made their way into the vast Northwest Territories they were faced with mile after mile of frozen snow and ice. The only transport available was the famous husky dog teams *these pages*. Though they are now being replaced, the huskies remain an important part of Arctic life.

When Whitehorse *opposite* was founded during the Klondike Gold Rush of 1897, it was a wild and lawless place. Today, however, it is the administrative capital of the Yukon Territory. Two thousand miles to the east lies Frobisher Bay on Baffin Island *this page*. The town has been designated as the center for education, administration and economic development for the eastern Arctic.

Perhaps the most enduring image of Canada is that of a land of ice and snow; this is nowhere more true than in the mountainous regions of the country. In the northern parts of Canada the land is in the grip of a terrible phenomenon, permafrost. This means that even during the summer, when the snows are melted, the ground remains frozen solid just a few inches beneath the surface. This inhibits the growth of any plants which require deep roots; only mosses and lichens can survive here. Even so the area supports a wide range of wildlife; dozens of species of birds and large herds of caribou inhabit this inhospitable land.

Surely the most awe inspiring natural sights in Canada are the mighty glaciers *above left* and *top left*. These vast, slow moving flows of ice and packed snow move remorselessly through the mountains grinding and scraping the bare rock into powder. Beneath their deceptively calm surfaces the glaciers carve out great 'U' shaped canyons in the rock and carry the debris down into the valleys where it can be washed away, so hastening the erosion of the mountains which will, nevertheless, take millions of years to achieve. Another odd natural wonder is the pingo. This is a giant block of ice which forms under the surface of the ground and forces the earth upwards until a large bulge in the landscape is created; some pingos may reach a height of 240 feet.

The city of Vancouver lies on the west coast of Canada, just north of the border with the United States. Its sheltered waters and favorable position have made it the largest port, in terms of freight handled, in Canada. Many passenger ships also sail from Vancouver: *bottom right* the Queen of the North, and *left* and *below* views of the city from the deck of the Prince George, leaving for Skagway.

The heavily indented coastline of British Columbia is washed by the warm Japanese Current. Where this warm water meets the cold arctic seas conditions are perfect for the tiny marine animals, known as krill, which are eaten by salmon, cod, halibut, herring and crabs. In their turn these fish and crustaceans are numerous off the coast. It is this combination of ocean currents which is responsible for the healthy fishing industry of the area.

Following the coastline of western Canada is a series of islands which vary in size from
the 250 mile long Vancouver Island *above* to tiny islets just a few feet across *opposite*.
These islands may lie as much as sixty miles offshore, creating a maze of sheltered
channels between them and the coast. Winding through this labyrinth is the famous
"Inside Passage," a deep water route from Vancouver to Alaska which is protected from
the large waves of the Pacific by the breakwater of islands.

Passengers on the Prince George *left*, *below* and *bottom*, which sails over 800 miles along the Inside Passage, are rewarded with magnificent views of mountain scenery including *opposite* the glacier at the end of Tracy's Arm. The Coast Mountains were formed millions of years ago as a result of titanic forces deep within the earth's crust.

Today, the famed Butchart Gardens in Victoria are a riot of color, but eighty years ago there was only a bleak quarry, owned by Robert Pim Butchart. Then Mr. Butchart, who was obviously a man of vision, decided to turn the quarry pit into a sunken garden. His hobby became almost an obsession, and today the Sunken Garden has been joined by Italian, Japanese and English Rose Gardens. Thousands of visitors come every year to marvel at this achievement.

The city of Vancouver *above* had its origins in a shantytown which sprang up round a
sawmill in 1862. By 1886 the population had grown to such an extent that the settlement
was incorporated as a city and named after Captain Vancouver, a Royal Naval Officer
who had charted the coast a century before. In the center of the city, Queen Elizabeth
Park contains the Bloedel Conservatory *right* which exhibits a large number of tropical
plants, including pineapples.

The bright lights of central Vancouver. On a small spit of land, between False Creek and Burrard Inlet, are crowded the high rise buildings which are the center of a bustling conurbation of over a million people. Once before the skyline of Vancouver has been aglow, but without the aid of electric light. One terrible day in June 1886 a great fire swept through the city and destroyed almost every building. But by the end of the year the stalwart citizens of Vancouver had rebuilt their city, and had wisely invested in their first fire engine.

The mountains and snows of British Columbia provide marvellous opportunities for the skier. There are many specially built ski resorts hidden away in the mountains, one of the most modern being Whistler Ski Village *above*. It is not only native Canadians who enjoy the slopes of British Columbia; Whistler Ski Village hosts the Molson World Downhill Championships. On the day of the contest the competitors ski down the hill carrying their nations' flags *opposite*.

Vancouver is a major financial, commercial and business center for western Canada and, like all such cities, has many fine hotels for visiting businessmen *above*. As the population of the city and its suburbs grew, it became increasingly obvious that a permanent road link was needed between West Vancouver, to the north of Burrard Inlet, and the city center, to the south. In 1938 this need resulted in the mighty Lions Gate Bridge across the mouth of the inlet *opposite*. This bridge, which is just under a mile long, carries thousands of vehicles every day and provides an essential crossing while still allowing shipping into the inlet.

The magnificent natural harbor of Burrard Inlet is the main reason for the prosperity of Vancouver. Its ability to provide a secure anchorage for cargo ships first attracted the loggers in 1862, while the railroad arrived in 1887. Today Burrard Inlet still provides freighters with a safe haven, but the smaller pleasure yachts find a mooring place in False Creek *above* and *opposite*. The entrance to this smaller harbor is crossed by a swingbridge which opens to allow yachts through and closes to allow the passage of trains.

The natural beauty of Vancouver's setting makes it a truly unique city. To the west the rolling blue ocean stretches into the distance, while to the east, precipitous mountains rise into the sky. Along the narrow strip of land between the two has grown up Canada's third largest city and her most important port.

Downtown Vancouver is the center of a bustling, modern commercial city. In common with many other important city centers large amounts of traffic rumble through its streets, but in Vancouver the numerous multi-laned roads *above* solve most of the problems. Lions Gate Bridge *opposite* has an ingenious three lane variable traffic system which ensures a smooth flow of traffic at all times of the day between West and Downtown Vancouver.

Sailing is a favorite pastime among Vancouver's residents. The numerous islands and
inlets along the coast make for excellent sailing waters and Vancouver Island protects
the area around the city from the worst of the Pacific rollers. Though many dozens of
yachts are moored in False Creek and Coal Harbor *opposite,* the Royal Vancouver Yacht
Club *above* is in Stanley Park, a thousand acre park set in the heart of the city.

Though Vancouver is essentially a commercial city, the more pleasurable side of life is not ignored. At Kitsilano Beach, on English Bay, there is a large swimming pool *above* and an attractive park in which stands engine 374, the railroad locomotive which pulled the first passenger train from Montreal in 1887. The MacMillan Planetarium *opposite* faces downtown Vancouver across False Bay. Projected onto its sixty-two foot dome are simulations of the night sky, which are accompanied by an interesting and informative talk.

The scenery of British Columbia is as beautiful as any to be found in Canada. Bowron Lake *opposite* gives its name to a 500 square mile Provincial Park. The Salish Indians of Horseshoe Bay *bottom right* amazed early explorers with the size of their cedar canoes.

In a country as vast and as diverse as Canada natural resources, not surprisingly, play an important part in the economy. In the early years of settlement men came to the wilderness areas to search for gold and silver, but the lodes quickly ran out and ghost towns mark the passing of the prospectors. Today another natural commodity, just as profitable as gold and potentially inexhaustable, pulls men to the untamed frontier: timber. Stretching right across northern Canada is a great belt of unbroken forest. This land, almost 1¾ million square miles in area, is one of the world's greatest concentrations of coniferous forest. Scattered across this vast expanse, amid the dramatic mountain scenery *opposite,* are numerous logging camps where trees are felled and stripped of their branches. Then, making use of the extensive system of rivers and lakes, the logs are floated or towed to large sawmills *this page* where the raw timber is processed into pulp, planks and beams before export. It is hardly surprising that Canadian timber production is consistently one of the highest in the world.

Lake Lillooet *above* is set amid magnificent mountain scenery, where trees and bushes grow in great profusion. Between the lake and Mount Currie runs an ancient Indian trail which, as the Lillooet Shortcut, became a famous goldrush route. The Skeena River *opposite* rises in northern British Columbia and winds through wide valleys and narrow canyons on its journey to the sea. In its upper reaches it passes 'Ksan, a restored Gitksan Indian village complete with painted cedar longhouses and totem poles.

Agriculture is an important feature of the British Columbian landscape, with many of the valley floors providing rich arable land. The Okanagan Valley is known as the "fruit basket of Canada," producing a third of all apples eaten in Canada as well as vast quantities of plums, pears, apricots and melons.

The awesome natural beauty with which they are surrounded *left, top* and *opposite* makes British Columbians aware of the pioneer heritage afforded them. At Fort Steele *above*, an 1890s town and fort has been reconstructed around the original, decaying ghost town. It was named after the legendary Mountie, Sam Steele, who established a police post on the site.

Some of the most spectacular driving in Canada is to be found on the seemingly endless gravel and dirt roads of the wilderness; but along with the beautiful scenery come many hazards. Flying gravel can damage lights, the radiator and the gastank, so it is advisable to have the car specially adapted before attempting these roads. Many of the roads are impassable in the winter, and some in the summer.

In the middle of the last century Barkerville *opposite* and *bottom right* typified the gold boom town. Today, after years of work, it has been restored to look as it did at the height of its prosperity. *Below, left* and *bottom left* is shown some of the excitement and action of the Prince George Professional Rodeo, held in June.

A statue of Captain Vancouver tops the dome of the Parliament Buildings *opposite* in
Victoria, the capital of British Columbia. Completed in 1898 the buildings were
constructed of local stone and seem to blend in with the gentle and endearing character
of the city. Victoria lives up to its name, being a very English and Victorian city; shops
sell tweeds and china, cricket is played in Beacon Hill Park and high tea can be obtained
in the Empress Hotel *above*.

Between the many gardens and parks of Victoria can be found the yacht harbor *above* and *opposite* and the house of J.S. Helmcken *top left*, who helped to negotiate the entry of British Columbia into the Confederation.

Edmonton *these pages* is not only the capital of Alberta, it is also the most northerly of Canada's major cities and because of this it may receive up to seventeen hours of sunlight each day in summer. This busy, thriving city stands on the banks of the North Saskatchewan River which flows into Lake Winnipeg.

Edmonton is a bustling, active city with a modern outlook on life, as is shown by its architecture and sculpture. The Muttart Conservatory *top left* is unlike any other in North America. Inside each of its numerous pyramids is a different controlled environment and climate. *Opposite* a desert climate inside one of the pyramids.

In the 1790s the Hudson's Bay Company set up a trading post on the bank of the North Saskatchewan River and called it Fort Edmonton. In less than two hundred years the trading post has grown into a city of more than 500,000 people which has the Provincial Legislative Buildings *top left* and a university *top right*. This growth is mainly the result of the Klondike Gold Rush.

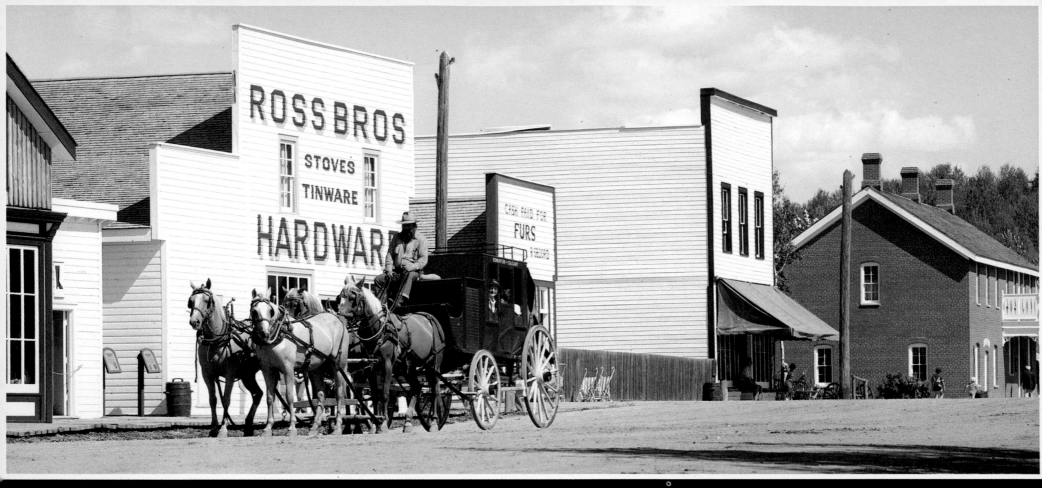

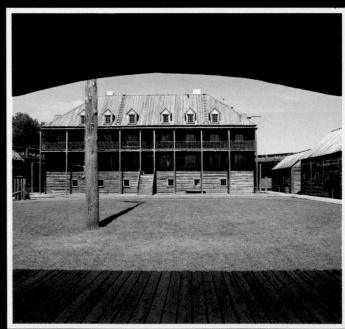

Modern Edmonton *far left* and *opposite* has come a long way from its days as a supply base for the Gold Rush. Those days are recreated at Fort Edmonton Park *left, above* and *top* which contains Rowlands House, built in 1840 *above*.

The city of Calgary is usually a peaceful place, containing the offices and banking facilities for the dozens of companies involved in the Canadian oil business. But every year, for ten days in July, the city holds its famous stampede, and steps back into history. Cowboys, real or drug store, come from all over Canada and the United States to compete for hundreds of thousands of dollars in prize money. Skills such as cattle wrestling and wild horse riding *these pages*, once essential to the cowboys' way of life, are practised for sport.

The great Calgary Stampede is ushered in by a spectacular parade through the city. Taking part are bands, majorettes, flag wavers and, of course, cowboys and Indians.

One of the perennially popular events at the Calgary Stampede is the musical ride of the Royal Canadian Mounted Police – the Mounties. Formed in 1873 to bring law and order to the wild North West Territories, the Mounties soon gained a reputation for toughness and a tradition of always getting their man. Though today they are a modern, fast-moving police force, the Mounties keep alive the precision horsemanship of days gone by in the Musical Drive.

In the days of the cowboy, skilful control of a horse was necessary for the management of the vast herds of cattle which had to be tended. Though today this control is sometimes taken to the extremes of circus riding *below* there remains enough of the rough and tumble *opposite, bottom left* **and** *bottom right* to give the Calgary Stampede a genuine flavor of the old West. The traditional Indian crafts of blanket weaving and feather headress making are on show at the Stampede and are for sale to the visitor.

Perhaps the most exciting of all the events held at Calgary during the Stampede is the chuckwagon race *these pages*. Once, the chuckwagon transported all the food and cooking utensils for cowboys during their long drives and to be a good cook also meant to be a good wagondriver. It is this dual expertise which lies at the root of the spectacular races in which four wagons, twenty riders and thirty-two horses gallop for the finish.

Calgary, a Gaelic name meaning "clear running water," is a bustling, zesty city
considered brash and pushy by the long established cities of eastern Canada. But it is
Canada's fastest growing city with thousands of people pouring in from all over the
country and a prosperity founded on oil. The skyline of modern Calgary is dominated by
the distinctive Calgary Tower *above* and *opposite* which stands some 620 feet tall and
houses an observation deck and a revolving restaurant.

Built on a tributary of the South Saskatchewan River, Calgary lies at the western edge of the Great Plains. Less than forty miles away, to the west, rise the first peaks of the mighty Rocky Mountain range, while to the east flat expanses of rich farmland stretch away to the horizon. Calgary owes its scenic setting to the discovery of oil in nearby Turner Valley in 1912.

In the extreme west of Alberta lies Medicine Lake *these pages,* so named because of its apparently magical properties. For much of the year the lake is a bed of dry gravel, but in the spring melting snow and ice fill the five mile long lake to a depth of fifty feet. During the summer the water then disappears, but there are no streams leaving the lake; the water seeps away through the gravel to join the Maligne River further downstream.

The effects of the seasons on mountain scenery can be seen quite clearly in these two pictures of Moraine Lake in the Valley of the Ten Peaks. The snow and ice of winter *above* lends a fairytale charm and elegance deceptively hiding the harshness of the mountain cold. The warmth of spring *opposite* melts the snows and brings a deep blue colour to the lake while the air begins to hum with the sounds of awakening life. From the lake a mile long path climbs to Sentinel Pass where picturesque subalpine meadows are dotted with spruce, fir and pine.

One of the prettiest sights in Banff National Park, or indeed in any mountain area, is Lake Louise in winter *these pages*. The curious milky green color of the lake is caused by sediments suspended in the water. Now one of the world's best known mountain views, Lake Louise was unknown to the civilised world until a Canadian Pacific Railroad workman, by the name of Tom Wilson, stumbled across it in 1882. It is now a popular center for climbing, hiking and riding.

The beautiful, silky waters of Peyto Lake *these pages* find their way down the mountains from Peyto Glacier. The lake and glacier are named after Bill Peyto, a respected mountain man and warden, who lived at the turn of the century. Just south of the lake is Bow Pass, which marks the watershed between the drainage basins of the North and South Saskatchewan Rivers. Waters that separate here will finally meet again near Prince Albert in central Saskatchewan, 500 miles away.

The Columbia Icefield *above left* covers a large area of the Canadian Rockies. Twelve of the twenty-five highest mountains are found in the icefield. Every day during the summer a fleet of glacier-travel vehicles operates from terminals to a point almost two miles up the Athabasca Glacier. It is from icefields and glaciers such as these that water melts in the spring to fill lakes *left* and *opposite* and to turn usually placid streams into raging torrents such as the Athabasca River *above*. The Athabasca was once the main route to the great North West. Barges would travel from the head waters near the Rockies via various staging posts to the Great Slave Lake and then down the Mackenzie River to the Beaufort Sea or the Yukon Gold Fields.

In the mountains of western Alberta meltwater streams are a common sight. As the
sunshine of spring and summer take their effect snow and glaciers melt, releasing
thousands of gallons of water which cascade down the mountains forming streams,
lakes and rivers. Eventually the running water draws together to form the great rivers of
the Plains: the Peace and the Athabasca which flow north and the Saskatchewan which
flows east to Hudson Bay.

Alberta is a province of great geographical diversity, which makes it of considerable interest to scientists. In the north of the province is a part of the Canadian Shield, an enormous and ancient slab of granite, hundreds of miles across, with a landscape characterized by thin soils and numerous lakes. In the southeast can be found the edge of the Great Plains *above left,* which stretch right across the continent to the Gulf of Mexico. But perhaps the most interesting region of Alberta is the mountain area in the southwest. Hundreds of millions of years ago the rocks which now form the mountains lay on the bottom of a shallow sea. The rocks formed at this time were sedimentary and in broad horizontal bands beneath the sea floor. When the powerful forces within the earth forced the rocks up to form the mountains, the bands of rock were bent and buckled. This process can be seen at its clearest at Mount Rundle near Banff *above* and *opposite.* It is quite clear that the horizontal rock strata have been tilted up at an angle of about thirty degrees and then eroded away to form the steeper slope. This type of mountain is known as a dipping layered mountain but there are many other types of mountain in Alberta.

The contrasting faces of water in Alberta. *Above* a peaceful sunset over a quiet lake, whose surface is barely rippled by a light evening breeze. *Opposite* the turbulent Athabasca River rushes past towering peaks near the start of its long run to the sea. At one point, known appropriately as Grand Rapids, the river level drops a dramatic thirty feet in just half a mile. It is surprising to find that, although water is of such importance to Alberta, it only covers about three percent of the province's area.

At the turn of the century, when the Canadian Government was encouraging settlers to populate the western provinces, bright posters advertised the prairies as "Canada West – The Last Best West." Farmers' sons from the east and newly arrived immigrants were lured west by the prospect of 160 acres of land for the price of ten dollars. The land the settlers found was wild and untamed but their success and that of their descendents can be seen in the rich landscape of rural Alberta *these pages.*

The Canadian Rockies is an area teeming with life. In the thick coniferous forests *above*, which cover hundreds of square miles, roam mountain caribou, black bears, grizzly bears, chipmunks, squirrels and dozens of species of bird, giving the area a rich and unique fauna. The lakes and rivers of the region *opposite* are also populated by a variety of living things. Trout swim through the crystal clear water, providing an important source of food and sport. For several weeks each year the rivers of the Pacific watershed come alive with salmon running up river to their spawning grounds, adding yet another facet to the rich picture of Rockies wildlife.

Regina, the capital of Saskatchewan, was once a settlement known as Wascana, from the Indian name meaning Pile of Bones, but in 1882 it was renamed in honor of Queen Victoria. The Indian name is, however, perpetuated in the Wascana Center, a 2,000 acre park set in the heart of the city. The imposing Legislative Building *top right* and *opposite* stands in this park. The modern City Hall is shown *above* and *top left*.

One of the major problems faced by the early settlers was the uncertainty of the water supply. Without a constant and steady supply crops such as wheat and sugar beet would simply die. The problem reached its greatest extent during the dustbowl years of the thirties. These catastrophic times made it obvious that something had to be done, so a series of irrigation projects was begun, culminating in the Gardiner Dam, completed in 1967 across the South Saskatchewan River, which has created a seventy-three mile long lake and has ensured a constant supply of irrigation water to the Saskatchewan fields *below left*. A new crop on the prairies is rape *left*. This remarkable plant yields a seed whose oil is used in products as diverse as varnish, ink, margarine, cooking oil and lubricating oil. Since 1960 production of rapeseed has tripled, helping to fill the grain silos of Saskatchewan *opposite*.

The great prairie lands of central North America are often referred to as the "Big Sky Country" because of the clear, uninterrupted view of the sky in all directions. The prairies of southern Saskatchewan are put to great use by the farmers of the region. They produce sixty percent of Canada's wheat, forty-five percent of her flax and fifty percent of her rapeseed. Unfortunately the people living in the area have to put up with great natural discomforts; temperatures can soar to 110° in the summer and plummet to 50° below in the winter, torrential rains and clouds of mosquitos also plague the population.

Over forty years after Manitoba became a province work began on the Legislative
Buildings *above* and *opposite* in Winnipeg, the provincial capital. The building took six
years, 1913-1919, to complete and was built in the classical Greek style. On top of the
dome was erected the famous Golden Boy, a gilded bronze statue of a running youth by
the French sculptor Charles Gardet. Within the building, flanking the grand marble
staircase, are two more famous sculptures; these are of Buffalos, an emblem of Manitoba.

To the earliest settlers in Manitoba, the great open plains were a great problem as well as a great opportunity. The heavy, though rich, soils and the extremes of weather were not at all like the European lands they had farmed before. It was not until the arrival of the Ukrainians and the Mennonites, with their experience of the Russian Steppes, that agriculture took a turn for the better. Today the sod huts and 160 acre plots of the early settlers are a thing of the past; large fields and vast farms have taken their place, making Manitoba one of the most efficient farming areas in North America.

Winnipeg began in 1812 as the Red River Settlement at the confluence of the Red and Assiniboine Rivers. The Settlement was established by Lord Selkirk, a well-known Scottish philanthropist, as a refuge for the thousands of crofters displaced during the infamous Clearances. Despite many early problems, not least the crofters unfamiliarity with prairie farming, the community prospered. In 1885 the railway came to Winnipeg, linking it to the east. The arrival of the railway was

of vital importance for the growing town; it transformed Winnipeg into the manufacturing and financial center of the west, a position it maintains to this day. While the old Legislative Building *left, above left* and *opposite* set against the modern city center indicates the respect felt by most Manitobans for the past, the starkly modern Royal Canadian Mint *above* typifies the bustling, go-ahead outlook of this city, whose half million strong population is continually increasing.

The prospect of open farmland *left* and *opposite* and the money to be made from associated industries *bottom right* and *bottom left* brought people to Manitoba from across the world. Many of these national groups stayed together, as with the Icelandic community at Gimli *below*.

Old Fort Henry *these pages* stands on a hill protectively overlooking the city of Kingston, Ontario, which was once the capital of Canada. The fort was built between 1832 and 1836 in preparation for a war with the United States which never occurred. Today the Fort Henry Guard parades every day, using drill and tactics authentic to the period in every detail, and fires salutes from the fort's original cannon *below*.

When construction of the St. Lawrence Seaway was in progress many old buildings were threatened. This opportunity was taken to move the buildings to one site, near Morrisburg, where a complete, working, nineteenth century village could be reconstructed. By contrast the Toronto City Hall *opposite*, built 1843, is one of the country's great classical buildings.

Reaching into the heart of the North American Continent is the famous Great Lakes-
St. Lawrence River System; *above* the St. Lawrence River near Johnstown and *opposite*
Millbay, Lake Superior. Not only has this network of waterways been of vital importance
to trade, but also to politics. The International Boundary between Canada and the
United States which runs through these waters has proved to be far more stable than the
frontier across the plains further west.

One of the most awe inspiring sights in Canada is that of hundreds of gallons of water cascading over the 150 foot drop at Niagara Falls. The first man to write of the Falls was Jean-Louis Hennepin in 1678, who called them a "prodigious cadence of water." Since 1800 honeymooners and holidaymakers alike have flocked to see the falls in their thousands to view the great beauty and grandeur of this natural wonder.

Whether by day or by night the business center of Toronto *these pages* reveals its dynamism for all to see. With the dramatic upward thrust of the office buildings it is clear that this is a place which is going somewhere. Indeed this city of three million souls is the nation's business and financial center and it is from this that the prosperity of Toronto stems.

The confidence in life and the future to be found in prosperous Toronto finds its most exciting expression in the modern architecture of the city. The soaring CN Tower *right* and *far right* seems to strain upwards for the sky and dominates the skyline. Its 1815 feet height, which makes it the tallest free-standing structure in the world, was built to transmit radio and television signals across the open plains. Such a building was necessary to make up for the lack of a convenient hill. In addition to the 300 foot transmission mast the tower contains two viewing platforms and a revolving restaurant which offers, apart from good food, stunning views of the city to diners. The new City Hall *top right*, completed in 1965 is another triumph of modern building. The gracefully curved twin towers partially encircle the saucer-shaped council chambers. In front of the City Hall can be seen the arched-over lake in Nathan Phillips Square; in winter this freezes and becomes a favorite skating venue for the city's people.

Every year since 1879 Toronto has hosted the Canadian National Exhibition *above* **which is held in Exhibition Park. The three week long "Ex" includes a livestock show, an agricultural fair and science, fashion and education displays, not to mention the diverse and exciting funfair. The "Ex," the oldest in the world, draws thousands of people to Toronto, which thereby lives up to its Indian name: "Place of Meeting." Being situated on Lake Ontario, Toronto has become a major focus for the fishing and sailing fraternities and has extensive private mooring facilities** *opposite.*

As a showpiece of Canadian industry, ingenuity and accomplishment Toronto cannot be equalled. The dramatic glass and stainless steel Royal Bank Plaza *above* rises above the prosperous financial district of Toronto. Ontario Place *opposite* is a futuristic mass of man-made islands, walkways and buildings on stilts. The large white dome is the Cinesphere which contains a curved cinema screen. The screen, at seventy feet wide and six stories tall, is the world's largest and can be viewed by 800 people at a time. The warship HMCS Haida is permanently moored at Ontario Place.

Toronto is famous for its excellent restaurants *left, below* and *bottom right* which not only provide a high level of cuisine but also reflect the traditions of the city's varied population. Casa Loma *bottom left* is a 98-room imitation castle built by industrialist Sir Henry Pellatt just before the First World War. Today the castle, complete with hidden panels, rooms and an underground tunnel, is open to the public.

The imaginative City Hall *opposite* is a continual source of pride for the people of Toronto. Its large forecourt is used for events as varied as rock concerts, brass bands and political soap-boxes. The Royal Bank Plaza, whose interior is shown *above*, demanded a quarter of a million dollars worth of gold leaf during its construction. The flag of Ontario flies alongside that of Canada *far right* outside Hydro Place, seen **again** *right* and *above right*.

Ottawa *above* and *opposite*, now the national capital of Canada, had very modest beginnings and its designation as the capital in 1857 came as a big surprise. In the early part of the last century Nicholas Sparks built a homestead here which remained isolated until the Rideau Canal arrived in 1826. At the time Ottawa was chosen by Queen Victoria it had grown into a lumbering village. The larger cities of Montreal, Toronto and Quebec were furious at the choice, deriding Ottawa as the "Westminster of the Wilderness," a name which has somehow stuck and become a source of pride for this businesslike capital.

It was inevitable that the Dominion Capital should borrow and adopt traditions from her parent capital. The Parliament Buildings *opposite* and *top right* and the uniforms and drill at the changing of the guard is similar to that of London.

Although the magnificent Parliament Buildings suffered extensive damage from fire in 1916 they were restored to their original Victorian Gothic design. The elaborate Senate Chamber *above* has a gilded ceiling and murals of the First World War line its walls. The less ornate House of Commons contains a replica of the Speaker's chair at Westminster. In the Confederation Hall *opposite* are pillars symbolizing the provinces and the Confederation.

Montreal *these pages* **stands at the heart of the St. Lawrence River, on an island which is 30 miles long and 9 miles wide. It is dominated by Mount Royal, a 750 foot high, extinct volcano. The city hums with activity, and a wander through the business areas and the port serves to confirm that this city is well and truly alive! The city is headquarters for four of Canada's great chartered banks, as well as for insurance and financial organisations and the Montreal Stock Exchange.**

The two great cities of Quebec; Montreal *left, bottom right* and *opposite* and Quebec *below* and *bottom left* contain many fine buildings. St. Joseph's Oratory *left* originated in 1904 when Brother André built a wooden chapel. The eight-sided dome of the basilica which now stands on the site is second in size only to St. Peter's, Rome. The world famous Chateau Frontenac *below* is a hotel.

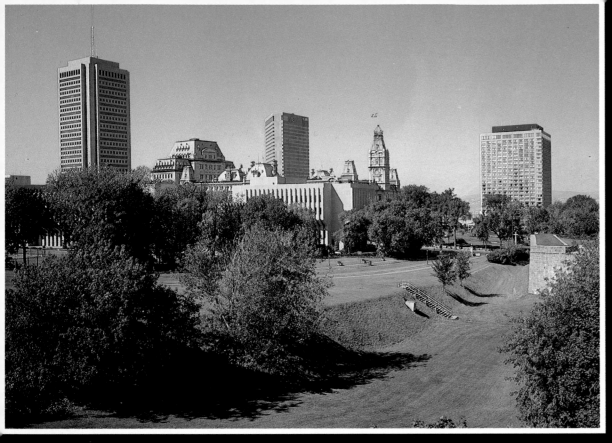

The traditional architecture of French Canada *left, above* and *top right* contrasts with the modern, less European architecture of today's Canada *left, top left* and *opposite,* but they merge together in the culture that is French Canada.

To the north of Montreal lies the Laurentian region, perhaps the most beautiful part of Quebec. Its unspoilt hills, forests and meadows are within easy reach of both Montreal and Quebec, providing a holiday playground for city dwellers.

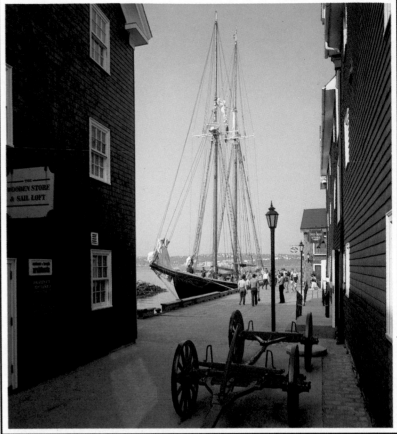

Halifax is not only the capital of Nova Scotia, it is also the largest seaport in the Atlantic Provinces. Its modern, containerized port facilities handle over three thousand ships a year. But amid all this hectic activity Halifax remembers its past. The *Bluenose II top right* **and** *top left* **makes trips around the harbor, and the streets where Captain Cook and General Monk walked still exist.**

Only about five percent of Nova Scotia's land is suitable for growing crops, and most of the agriculture is based on livestock, poultry and dairy farming. Fishing is a major activity and the province has many lovely fishing villages like Peggy's Cove *these pages*. Shellfish, haddock and cod are the main catches.

The people who live in the many small fishing villages scattered along the coast of Nova Scotia do not confine their activities to catching fish. The oysters from Malpeque Bay are considered by many to be the best in the world, an opinion shared by those who catch them. Aficionados usually shuck their Malpeques and eat the oyster raw. It is said that no lobster ever dies of old age, and given the relentless pursuit of these delectable creatures it is no wonder. Many lobsters are eaten in Nova Scotia while others are shipped south. Peggy's Cove *these pages* is a very typical Nova Scotian fishing village. It is extremely popular with visitors who come to see its spindle-legged dock, its weathered boats, its bleached rocks and its attractive lighthouse.

In the northeastern part of Nova Scotia can be
found Cape Breton Island on which these pictures
were taken: *above* and *opposite* Neils Harbour, *top
left* St. Peter's and *right* and *top right* the
reconstructed fortress of Louisbourg.

In the Annapolis Valley, during the eighteenth century, lived a group of French farmers, known as Acadians. Their rich farmlands became a target in one of the many wars between France and England and, as a result, they were forced to leave in 1755 for lands in New England. But the Acadians did not accept this sudden change and slowly made their way back home. The first to arrive was Joseph Dugas in 1768, having walked the full 300 miles. Many more followed and today most of the people in villages, such as Sandford *above* and Cape St. Mary *opposite,* on Nova Scotia's west coast, are of Acadian ancestry.

From the traditional weatherboard houses, *right* in Mahone Bay, townsfolk await the return of menfolk in the fishing boats *top left* and *opposite*. Two centuries ago they would have had more cause to worry, for Nova Scotia suffered from raids by French, Spanish and United States privateers.

During the last century, when vast numbers of wooden ships plied the oceans, Nova Scotia had one of the largest fleets of all, more than 3,000 windjammers. An inexhaustible supply of timber, and tough sailors from small villages, as on *these pages,* made the Bluenose fleet, as Nova Scotians were known, the envy of the Atlantic coast. Yarmouth, the fleet's base, was the richest port per capita on the coast.

The Kings Landing Historical Settlement, near Prince William New Brunswick, *these pages* recreates life as it was some 150 years ago for the early settlers. Parlors *below*, nurseries *bottom right* and kitchens *bottom left* are restored and the General Store *left* only sells contemporary goods.

Many of the 60 buildings at Kings Landing
Historical Settlement *these pages* have been
relocated from sites in other parts of the Province.
The Kings Head Inn *top right* still serves draft beer
and eighteenth century fare.

The costumed staff at Kings Landing keep many of the working buildings in running order; *below* a waterfall and *bottom right* a blacksmith's forge, lending an air of authenticity to the settlement.

With all the natural beauty of the New Brunswick countryside, *opposite* at Point Wolfe, it is easy to see why the Acadians were so keen to return in 1755. Their way of life is recreated at the Acadian Historical Village *right*, **below** and *bottom left*.

A feature of the Canadian
coast is the abundance of
smooth, sandy beaches which,
during the summer, attract
crowds of people with their
irresistible blend of sun and
sea. All along the coastlines of
New Brunswick, Prince Edward
Island, Nova Scotia and
Newfoundland can be found
sheltered coves with golden
beaches. They are not all safe
to swim from, however,
dangerous undercurrents can
drag the unwary out to sea and
violent storms can quickly
blow up. But whether the sea is
calm or tumultuous these
shores have a charm all their
own as can be seen *these pages.*